Juan Rafael Juarez Díaz
Efraín de la Cruz Bardalez Zapata
Llanice Chota Riva

Speaking English to High School Students

Juan Rafael Juarez Díaz
Efraín de la Cruz Bardalez Zapata
Llanice Chota Riva

Speaking English to High School Students

Comparison between public and private education students

ScienciaScripts

This book is a translation from the original published under ISBN 978-620-0-39398-2.

Publisher:
Sciencia Scripts
is a trademark of
International Book Market Service Ltd., member of OmniScriptum Publishing Group
17 Meldrum Street, Beau Bassin 71504, Mauritius
Printed at: see last page
ISBN: 978-620-0-86853-4

Speaking English
in high school students

AUTHORS

Juan Rafael Juarez Diaz

Efrain de la Cruz Bardalez Zapata

Llanice Chota Riva

Tarapoto - Peru

2020

Index

Summary

The research work called: **Level of oral expression of the English language in students of a public and private educational institution, 2019,** had as a general objective, to determine the differences in the level of oral expression of the English language between students of a public educational institution and private institution, 2019., for which the descriptive comparative design was used, working with a two sample, 28 students of the private institution and 30 estudaitnes in the public institution.

For the collection of data on the study variables, the questionnaire was used to measure the level of oral expression of the English language. Also, the information collected was systematized by means of descriptive statistics through statistical tables and graphs, which allowed us to arrive at conclusions and recommendations.

It was found that the private institutions have a higher level of oral expression of the English language, in the very good level it is presented with 32.14%, unlike the students of the public EI where the level of very good oral expression is only 9.38%. In the good level, the comparison is 39.29% for the private institution and 20.31% for the public educational institution. The level of oral expression of the English language in students of a public educational institution, 2019; the most predominant is the regular level with 37.50%. The level of oral expression of the English language in students of a private educational institution, 2019, is the level with 39.9%, which indicates that the students present better conditions in the articulation of words. The very good level is at 32.14% and the regular level at 17.86%,

KEY WORDS: Oral expression level, mastery of speech, fluency and comprehension.

Abstract

The research work called: Level of oral expression of the English language in students of a public and private educational institution, 2019, had the general objective of determining the differences in the level of oral expression of the English language between students of a public educational institution and institution Privada, 2019., for which the comparative descriptive design was used, working with two samples, 28 students from the private institution and 30 students at the public institution.

To collect data on the study variables, the questionnaire was used to measure the level of oral expression in the English language. Likewise, the information collected was systematized using descriptive statistics through statistical tables and graphs, allowing the results to be reached to arrive at the conclusions and recommendations.

It was found that private institutions have a higher level in oral expression of the English language, at the very good level it is presented with 32.14%, unlike the students of public EI where the level of very good oral expression is only of 9.38%. At the good level, the comparison is evident in 39.29% for the private institution and 20.31% for the public educational institution. The level of oral expression of the English language in students of a public educational institution, 2019; the most predominant is the regular level with 37.50%. The level of oral expression of the English language in students of a private educational institution, 2019, is at the level with 39.9%, which indicates that the students present better conditions in articulation of words. The very good level is at 32.14% and the regular one with 17.86%,

KEY WORDS: Level of oral expression, command of speech, fluency and comprehension.

Introduction

Teaching oral communication is a challenge for teachers in the area of language teaching. One reason may be that in most cases the student has no way to practice this language skill outside of the English class. Also, in some cases, this skill is not given enough time to practice; or the activities are not appropriate for that purpose.

The assessment of oral competence is one of the most subjective in the teaching of a second language and sometimes the one that causes the most conflict in terms of fair and unfair assessment depending on the objectives of that assessment. In addition to the problem of subjectivity, there is the complexity of the time required to carry out the activity individually, the preparation of the activity, the specific heading to be used and the requirements of the process or protocol that should be followed for correct assessment. (Pompous, 2016).

Communicative competence in the English language has increased worldwide due to sociolinguistic factors. Those who learn a language have also changed, so the teaching of English has diversified, making it available to majority groups of the population through a series of reforms. Therefore, a wide variety of resources and opportunities are available for language immersion in a globalized society (Bakken & Lund, 2018).

According to UNESCO, in the section on languages and multilingualism, it states that languages play a key role in development by ensuring cultural diversity and intercultural dialogue, strengthening cooperation, building inclusive knowledge societies and preserving cultural heritage, in order to apply the benefits of science and technology for sustainable development (UNESCO, 2016).

Many communicative factors are involved in the assessment of oral competence, since oral communication involves the negotiation of meanings between two or more people in a given context (O'Malley and Pierce, 1996). These factors are not only linguistic, such as pronunciation, grammar, fluency or comprehension, but pragmatic, making the oral message effective from a communicative point of view, especially in professional contexts.

One of the difficulties in the development of communicative competence in English is the incipient application of active methods in the teaching of the English language. On this aspect, the authors Richards and Rodgers describe that the theoretical basis of Communicative Language Teaching has a great eclectic flow; and express that the objective of English teaching is communication (Richards and Rodgers, 2008 p.155).

This project was born out of the author's concern to observe that students still have difficulty communicating in the target language when they finish their courses. This idea was confirmed when she made some observations and when she listened to the teachers' comments, who said that the students do not learn to communicate orally, and on their side the students mentioned the difficulty of being able to interact in this language. It was then decided to carry out a study to help document the situation in an objective manner by obtaining information that once analysed would provide data that would help to change a situation.

All this has resulted in poor English language skills among students in both public and private schools.

The problem is posed as follows: What is the difference between the level of oral expression of the English language among students in a public educational institution and a private institution, 2019? What is the level of oral expression of the English language among students in a public educational institution, 2019? What is the level of oral expression of the English language among students in a private educational institution, 2019?

The research is justified because it allowed to explain the comparison between the education in a private school and a public one, about the development of the oral expression in English and how they help in the process of acquisition of the English or foreign language. Because it is a topic that has been talked about a lot but applied little in practice, the contribution it made is imperative, since most professionals are unaware of all the advantages that can be drawn from it. By finding the difference between the two populations, oral expression can be promoted among students in public institutions where the lowest level is found, which is not only important for the students, but also for the parents and the community.

People who are in the process of learning a second language can get a lot of benefits and enjoy them and consequently the whole strenuous process that demands communicating in another language will go unnoticed. The significance of the results allows for clarification regarding the development of a foreign language, due to the purpose of trying to apply a more communicative model according to the differences that may be found in some of the samples.

The objective of the research is to determine the differences in the level of oral expression of the English language between students of a public educational institution and a private institution, 2019. . To identify the level of oral expression of the English language in students of a public educational institution, 2019. To identify the level of oral expression of the English language among students in a   private   educational institution, 2019. This research is organized according to the following chapters:

In chapter I; all the bibliographical review related to both study variables in the research background and theoretical bases are presented. In chapter **II, the** materials and methods are grouped according to the system of variables, the research hypotheses, the type of method, the research design and the population and sample; in **chapter III, the research** results are presented, which for the present research are at a descriptive level and at a correlational level using statistical instruments and tables and graphs, as well as the discussion of the results. Finally, the conclusions and recommendations resulting from the research are presented, as well as the bibliography consulted and some annexes considered to be important for the development and presentation of this thesis.

CHAPTER I

BIBLIOGRAPHIC REVIEW

1.1. Background to the investigation

At the international level

Navarro. H: and Zarate, W. (2016). Colombia. In their thesis entitled "Difficulties presented by students in the oral production of English in the fifth grade of primary school at Max Planck High School". The objective of this study was to identify the educational conditions that limit the oral production of English in the area of the fifth grade students of the Max Planck High School in Usme, Yomasa. It follows the descriptive method, in which three instruments were used to collect information, namely: two questionnaires addressed to 35 fifth-grade primary school students and an interview conducted with the English teacher. For the analysis of the data obtained, the simple statistical method was used, which made it possible to identify: 1) students have limitations in solving real-life communicative tasks, according to their educational level; 2) they avoid the verbalised use of the English language for fear of ridicule and making mistakes; 3) the different educational activities, whose purpose is progress and mastery in the area of English, show a serious interruption and an intermittent flow that make it impossible to apprehend knowledge. Therefore, as a closing remark, it was considered pertinent to propose some alternatives that could contribute to the improvement of their performance in the oral production of English.

Fuertes, N; Escudero, I; Armijos, J and Loaiza, E. (2018). Ecuador. In the research called "Synergy of active methods in oral expression, grammar and vocabulary in students of English as a foreign language". The objective was to design a methodological proposal to develop oral expression in English in undergraduate students. Methodologically it was quantitative type, quasi-experimental design, without random assignment, longitudinal cut. Two experimental and control groups were compared with pre and post intervention evaluation. The sample, 50 students from the Language Center, National University of Chimborazo. For data collection and analysis a test was designed and the U of Mann-Whitney was applied.   It was determined that the Synergy of active methods improved the development of oral expression, grammar and vocabulary. According to the results it is concluded that the application of the synergy of active methods acts in a more effective way in the development of grammar because of the emphasis that the active methods make in using this sub skill as a communicative resource and not as a cognitive resource as the traditional methods do; that is to say, that grammar is developed by setting a context and communicative purpose.

Bañuelos, C. (2014). Mexico. A study on the oral production of the English language. Its purpose is to identify the methodology used in the classroom regarding the development of oral communication. For the observations, 7 groups of the English courses of the Faculty of Languages were taken into account, one group of each level, of the 7 that make up the total course. One observation per group was made during one semester. The instrument of the observations consisted of sixteen reagents planned to detect the type of methodology carried out by the teacher in the class. It was concluded that the teaching of a language and its efficiency depends partly on the ability to understand the methodology being used and the effects it can have on the students and their needs. If, on the one hand, the primary need of the student is to communicate orally, then opportunities must be provided for him/her to develop this ability, focusing on language as a means of communication, and that this has the purpose of giving the student something to say when he/she needs it, helping the student to use the different functions of the language from the first levels.

Ramírez, B. (2017). Ecuador. In his thesis to obtain the professional title, called "The linguistic games for the development of the oral expression of the English language in the students of the secondary section of the New Vision School in the period 2015 - 2016". It presents as an objective to analyze how the linguistic games helped in the development of the oral expression of the English language, the characteristics in general were based on the development of phonetic, phonological, lexical, semantic, syntactic morph and stylistic components of the language and in a more specific way they were centered in sub skills like: verbal fluency, precision, rhyme and memorization. Therefore, a basic research line was pursued, that is, without a practical purpose, but that sought to increase the knowledge of the fundamental principles oriented to the application. Likewise, this study was non-experimental since it was carried out without deliberately manipulating the variables, it was based on the observation of the phenomenon in its natural context and therefore it was a descriptive field research. The population investigated was not large, so it was not necessary to use a sample and the population as a whole was evaluated. What was used as an instrument was the questionnaire which measured the frequency with which language games are used within the school classroom. In addition, it was also analyzed how other linguistic, paralinguistic and extralinguistic elements play a fundamental role when students express themselves orally, allowing the teacher to have a broader conceptual and cognitive vision when applying techniques that allow the development of oral English expression.

Guamán, V. (2014). Whose theme is: Verbal games and their impact on the oral expression of children in the first, second and third grades of the "Carlos María de la Condamine" private school in the city of Ambato, Tungurahua province: Final report on the graduation work prior to obtaining the degree of Bachelor of Education. Mention: Basic Education. UTA. 123 p. Results found: Verbal games allow the development of the ludic and creative function of oral language, as well as the linguistic awareness, its progressive characteristics in the different age levels and its social environment. The author focused his research on how verbal games allow the student to develop mental structures such as linguistic awareness and how this is applied according to the age level and the socio-educational environment in which the student is immersed.

At the national level:

Palma, E. and Zapata, C. (2017). In the research titled "Methodological strategies to improve oral expression in the English area, of the 3rd grade students of the I.E.E. "Juan Manuel Iturregui" - Province of Lambayeque". Its objective was to propose methodological strategies to improve oral expression, in the area of English, of the students of the 3rd grade of secondary school of the Emblematic Educational Institution "Juan Manuel Iturregui" of the District of Lambayeque, Province of Lambayeque- Lambayeque Region. It presents as conclusions that in the diagnosis made, it is concluded that 87% of students of the third grade of secondary, show a low level of oral expression, as evidenced in the results. The learning sessions were developed taking into account the different methodological strategies, which led us to improve oral expression.   The proposals were considered taking into account the socio-cultural theories and the social cognitive theory of Bandura

Álvarez and Panta (2017) in their thesis called the application of the role play technique to improve the oral expression of the English language in students in the fifth year of secondary school at the Manuel Muñoz Najar Educational Institution, Arequipa - 2016, whose objective is to identify if the application of the role play technique will improve the level of oral expression in students in the fifth year of secondary school at the Manuel Muñoz Najar Educational Institution. According to the results obtained, the author concluded that in pronunciation, fluency, comprehension and command of the speech of the oral expression of the English language in the control group, according to the post-test, indicate that there was some improvement in oral expression, placing the students in the low levels of evaluation that is to say in the regular and bad levels. The results of the post test regarding the levels of oral expression in each one of its dimensions: pronunciation, comprehension, fluency and command of the speech, revealed an important difference between the control group and the experimental group, so we have that in the experimental group the results in pronunciation reached the highest levels: excellent, (35.71%); very good, (35.71%) and good (28.57%).

Leon. G. (2014). Participatory techniques to improve the oral expression of the English language. Case: mechatronics students from SENATI, de la Esperanza-Trujillo. Academic cycle 2013-II. The aim was to demonstrate its influence on oral expression. It was postulated that the application of participatory techniques improves the oral expression of the English language. Following a quasi-experimental design, a pre and post-test was applied, establishing five levels of evaluation: excellent, very good, good, regular and bad. The results of the evaluation in pronunciation, fluency, comprehension and command of the speech, of the experimental group, were located in the highest levels and showed significant differences ($p < 0.05$) with respect to those of the control, according to the post-test. The global average of oral expression in the experimental group, according to the post-test was 16.86 and in the pre-test 11.00. The comparison of the averages showed significant differences ($p < 0.05$), as was also obtained by comparing the overall averages between the experimental group and the control. It is concluded that the participatory techniques significantly improved the learning of the oral expression of the English language.

Mamani, E. (2016). Cooperative learning as a strategy in the development of oral expression in English in students of the Tourism School of UNA Puno 2016. This research had as objective the effectiveness that produces the cooperative learning as a strategy in the development of the oral expression in English in the students of the Professional School of Tourism of the National University of the Altiplano of Puno in the year 2016. This work is justified because it is subject to the application of active methodological strategies, apart from improving oral expression in the English language, the technical-pedagogical work of the teachers has been improved by knowing their strengths and weaknesses, in such a way that the teachers who work at the Professional School of Tourism now have a source of information which serves as a basis for generating other research related to the topic. The research hypothesis was: the effects produced by cooperative learning as a strategy is of significant improvement in the development of oral expression in the students researched. Through the type of quasi-experimental research with two groups of pre and post test, to a sample of 65 students in which it has been possible to arrive at the following conclusions: That the students, managed to reach high levels (good and very good) in the development of their oral expression abilities, product of the application of the cooperative learning, this in the experimental group, while in the control group, the students remain in the levels of regular and good, the test of hypothesis of the difference of means and the distribution of (Zc), evidences this conclusion as analysis of the results obtained the Zc= 3,66, the arithmetic means: 15,4 in the experimental group and 12.8 of the control group in the exit test.

Quispe, W. (2017). Oral English language proficiency in third grade students at El Mártir José Olaya de Ventanilla educational institution, 2016. The objective was to determine the level of oral English language proficiency among third grade students at the El Mártir José Olaya de Ventanilla educational institution; in this way we set out to discover how students perform orally when they learn a foreign language. The population was made up of the students of the third grade of the aforementioned institution, of which the 49 students of sections A and B were intentionally sampled as a census sample; and the instrument called "English Language Comprehension and Oral Expression Test" was applied, which was previously submitted to expert judgment for validation, and to the KR20 test to pass its reliability. Methodologically, our research is of a descriptive type, which belongs to a basic level and was developed with a simple descriptive method, taking the transversal design that belongs to the non-experimental design, with a quantitative approach. Once the informative data on the oral competence of the English language and its dimensions were collected, we continued to find the statistical results, for which it was necessary to rely on the SPSS version 23 program, which allows us to specify in detail the results of the levels of the variable and its dimensions. Finally, we concluded that students in the third grade of secondary school at the El Mártir José Olaya de Ventanilla educational institution develop oral English language skills in a less than optimal manner; what they do best is to understand the language, but they have greater difficulty in expressing themselves orally.

Aspajo (2014), in his thesis for the degree in Techniques to develop the capacity for oral expression and comprehension in the learning of the English language in students of the second grade of secondary school in Colegio No. 029 in Yurimaguas, presented at the Universidad Nacional de la Amazonia Peruana, Iquitos, 2014, posed the problem of how to develop the capacity for oral expression and comprehension in the area of English in students of the second grade of secondary school in Colegio No. 029 in Yurimaguas in 2013. The sampling was probability-based and worked with a sample of 59 students. With the application of the pretest to evaluate the students' oral expression and comprehension, it was found that they are between the levels of poor and poor, without finding participants in the levels of regular, good and very good.

Palomino, K; Polo, R .and Sedano, J. (2015). In the research entitled: Los medios educativos y la expresión y comprensión oral del inglés en los estudiantes del tercer grado de secundaria del colegio experimental de aplicación de la Universidad nacional de educación Enrique Guzmán y Valle, Chosica, 2015. This research demonstrated the correlation between educational media and the oral expression and comprehension of English in third grade students at the Enrique Guzmán y Valle National University of Education's Experimental Application College, Chosica, 2015. The study was non-experimental, substantive, cross-sectional and of descriptive-correlational design. The sample was made up of 51 third grade students registered in 2015. The instruments used were an educational media questionnaire and an oral expression and comprehension test. The results obtained confirmed, based on Pearson's statistical correlation analysis, that there is a significant relationship between the study variables. In this sense, teachers should be trained in the use of educational media to improve oral expression and comprehension.

1. 2. Theoretical basis

Communicative Competence

This method gives importance to the communicative process and to the relationships established between the subjects who interact. It works with integrated skills (oral production, written production, listening and reading).

It seeks to ensure that authentic language plays a major role and, moreover, that it develops in real contexts. The activities are intended to produce information and promote real communication interactions.

Richard & Rodgers (2001) state that the communicative approach was developed due to the criticism of the methods used previously -Audiolingual and Situational Language Teaching- and also due to the changing educational realities in Europe.

Littlewood (1994) points out that students must learn to use language spontaneously and flexibly to express their message and must be in situations where they must use language as a tool for their communication needs and where the criterion for success is functional efficiency rather than structural accuracy. Thus, the teaching of communicative languages in real-life situations that require communication.

"The most efficient communicator in a foreign language is not always the person who is best at manipulating its structures. He is often the person who is most adept at processing the entire situation involving himself and his environment by taking into account the language already shared between them, and selecting elements that will communicate his message effectively. Foreign language learners need opportunities to develop these skills, situations in which emphasis is placed on using their resources by communicating meanings as efficiently and economically as possible" (Littlewood, 1994, p. 4).

The aim is to "free activity from dependence on the teacher so that students begin to interact as equal partners in an exchange" (Richards & Rogers, 2001, p.12).

The role of the teacher during these activities can be: a group process manager, a facilitator, a counsellor (answering questions and monitoring the activity), a participant within the group. Richards & Rodgers (2001) summarize the contributions of this method:

- Provides "full task practice" (total skill)
- Improves motivation
- Allows for natural learning
- It can create a context that supports learning.

Communicative competence, the main objective of language learning, can be sustained through various techniques given especially by the Communicative Approach.

Oral Communication

Oral communication involves the production of various oral texts, and listening comprehensively to the implicit and explicit messages of different interlocutors, in order to achieve optimal communication. This involves recognizing and using verbal, non-verbal and para-verbal resources in various communication situations. (Ministry of Education, 2017)

In oral communication, the interlocutors can alternate the condition of listener and speaker in order to construct oral texts in a variety of communicative situations, which implies that they are capable of adapting their language according to the context.

The progression of learning on this map is described by considering two competencies, each of which becomes more complex at different levels:

Oral comprehension. This competence describes the understanding of different oral texts, recognizing and infusing the meanings. It also describes the speaker/listener's distance from oral texts produced by others, in a reflective way, in order to analyse and assess them, based on the context in which they are produced and understood. This involves developing the following:

Identify explicit information from the oral texts you hear.

Infer and interpret the speaker's intention from the use of non-verbal and para-verbal resources.

Infer and interpret the theme, purpose and conclusions of the oral texts you hear.

Reflect on the oral text of your interlocutor by comparing and contrasting it with your knowledge and experiences in relation to the context.

Oral production. This competence describes the production of speeches by a speaker, as well as the collaborative1 production of various types of oral texts to interact directly (face to face) or through a technological support (teleconferences, video calls, etc.), in a spontaneous or structured way. It also includes the use of non-verbal and para-verbal resources, as well as the exchange of roles (sender-receiver) according to the communicative situation.

This involves developing the following:

Adapt to the communicative situation, which implies keeping in mind the addressee, the purpose, the context and the register.

Express ideas in a coherent and cohesive way.

Use a varied vocabulary.

Use non-verbal and para-verbal resources appropriately.

Ask the speaker appropriate questions and make contributions that lead to clarification of the speech. (SINEACE, 2013)

Importance of oral expression

Of all skills, oral production is intuitively the most important: people who master a language are referred to as "speakers" of that language, Ur wrote. P. (1996) in his book "A Course in LanguageTeaching". He also states that productive skills are based on students feeling the necessary confidence and being able to express themselves freely without fear of making mistakes. Homework is an excellent opportunity for students to develop confidence and experience communicating with both their teacher and their peers. It also allows students to make a meaningful assimilation of everything they have learned in class and need to apply and process it in their mother tongue before they feel comfortable expressing it in the English language. According to Fonseca (2005), today's society demands an efficient communicative capacity in which people know how to express themselves fluently and clearly, with optimum pronunciation and intonation, and that they use pertinent and natural non-verbal resources (mime, gestures, body movement) that make themselves heard but also listen to others. The teaching of oral communication must be presented in formal and informal situations, which is why it is proposed to develop skills for conversation, dialogue, debate, storytelling, oral reporting, among other forms of oral communication. Today's society demands efficient communication skills. The possibilities for work, study, social relations and self-improvement depend, to a large extent, on our ability to interact with others, having oral expression as a fundamental tool. It is therefore necessary to contribute to the strengthening of the target language, especially in the following aspects

Correct articulation, so that the pronunciation of the sounds is clear

Intonation appropriate to the nature of the speech.

Fluency in the presentation of ideas.

Proper use of gestures and mimicry.

Persuasiveness

Clear expression of ideas.

Oral expression

Byrne (1989) defines oral expression as a double process, or two-way process between the speaker and the listener, where the productive ability of oral expression and the receptive ability of listening are present, producing a process of interpretation and negotiation of meanings.

Vigotsky (1987) states that oral expression is an exchange of thoughts and emotions. They affirm that the human being evolves in a historical-cultural context where communication plays an outstanding role related to daily activity since man faces a constant interaction with his fellow men in society, having communication as a fundamental premise.

When speaking of oral expression, the curricular bases of English contemplated by the MEN (2012) conceive it as "a productive ability of English that involves using the language to communicate ideas orally. Oral expression consists of communicating a message with appropriate pronunciation and in an intelligible manner by participating in oral exchanges, conversations and monologues" (p. 229).

Oral expression is one of the four basic skills that are developed in the acquisition of both the mother tongue, unconsciously, and a foreign or second language, consciously or unconsciously. In addition, it is the act of being able to express feelings, ideas or desires that a person possesses through language. Oral expression is born due to the need of people to be able to communicate their desires, feelings and emotions, so it is vital to be able to develop this skill when one intends to learn a second or foreign language, since that is the interest of learning it, not only understanding it, but rather being able to express what one wants.

Medina (2012), an academic in the field of language teaching, states that "oral expression is a process through which the student, a speaker in interaction with one or more people and in an active manner, plays the double role of receiving the message of the interlocutor(s) and codifying their message, with the aim of satisfying their communicative needs in the foreign language", therefore, the ability to use a language, in this case English as an L.E, This is not only about the enunciation and/or transmission of a message, but also about the relationships existing in the communicative act, it is about the different perspectives between two or more actors with two or more possibly antagonistic worlds, with different ideologies, it involves a bilateral or in many cases multilateral link, and this is the importance of the proper use of the language for the student, who should approach the language, not with the fear of failure, but with the attitude of the one who learns not in spite of but through the mistakes.

In Speaking the Common European Framework of Reference for Languages states that the ability to speak includes 2 categories: oral production and oral interaction; in oral production activities, oral texts are produced for an audience. In interaction activities, the speaker acts alternatively with one or more other speakers through negotiation and monitoring of meaning, using both the cooperative and conversational principle (Council of Europe, 2001).

According to Bygates (1991) it is the ability to assemble sentences in the abstract, which are produced and adapted to the circumstances of the moment. That is, making quick decisions, integrating them properly, and adjusting them according to unexpected problems that appear in different types of conversation.

On the other hand, Brown and Yule (1983), who consider that oral production is an interactive process where a meaning is constructed that includes producing and receiving, as well as processing information. Form and meaning depend on the context where the interaction takes place, including the participants, their experiences, the environment and the purpose of communication. It is often spontaneous, has beginnings and endings, and has a development.

For many students, oral expression is the most difficult skill in learning the target language. Traditionally, four language skills have been discussed, two from the oral language, namely listening comprehension and speaking, and two from the written language, namely reading comprehension and writing. The two comprehension skills are correlated, as are the two expression skills; however, in both cases the skills are as different as the oral and written languages are different. The European Framework of Reference mentioned, on the one hand, listening and reading comprehension as receptive language activities and, on the other hand, oral expression and written expression as productive language activities.

Speaking activities

According to Harmer (2000), oral communication activities should incorporate a communicative purpose or intention that provokes the student to engage in the various oral exchanges. Similarly, the teacher may, through an oral activity, involve the student not only in the oral coding of a message, but also in the different aspects of the spoken language such as pronunciation practice or other aspects such as intonation or stress. The typology of activities for the practice of oral production is very varied and each teacher has his or her own preferences. Therefore, we will deal with the most expanded activities or techniques of this communicative skill by including them in three groups

Pair work: Pair work offers students the opportunity to "think out loud" as they go through a process of acquiring and reflecting on the information they have been given. The most commonly used exercises for pair work are the so-called "Information / Communication gap activities". In this type of activity each student has a series of data that the other student does not have, the main objective of this activity being to ask questions to obtain the information that is not possessed.

Puzzles or "Jigsaw Activities": the purpose of this type of activity is identical to that of "Information/ Communication gap", with the difference that the puzzles are more elaborate and several students can participate. In a jigsaw activity each student has one or more pieces of the puzzle and must cooperate communicatively to fit all the pieces into place.

Discussions: Discussions are an effective activity for the use of oral language. We can organize students into groups to reach agreement on a topic. In order for a discussion to be effective and lead to the student's learning, it is necessary for the teacher to prepare the discussion beforehand.

Simulations or 'role plays': Simulations are excellent for students to use all their communication resources in simulated communication situations. In this activity, the teacher assigns each student a role within a fictional situation. Therefore, the student will have to use the language in accordance with the communicative situation. Simulations, apart from being ideal for language practice, are a way of promoting sociolinguistic competence, since the students establish social relationships during the development of the activity.

Dimensions of oral expression

Thornbury (2006), tells us that according to the Cambridge Certificate in English Language Speaking Skills (CELS) - Speaking Test - there are four dimensions considered for the evaluation of oral expression.

Pronunciation: Refers to the student's ability to produce understandable statements based on individual sound production, appropriate logical connection of words, and the use of stress and intonation to convey intended meaning.

Comprehension: A component of oral expression that assesses the ability to integrate the explicit implications and meanings of words and sentences in spoken language. This skill includes auditory attention, memory and perception, as well as actual comprehension.

Fluency: Refers to the ability to speak with ease and spontaneity. The student speaks coherently using appropriate sentence length speed.

Speech Mastery: Component of oral expression that evaluates the ability to express ideas and opinions in a coherent and logical discourse using accurate and complex structures according to different statements or situations.

1.3. Definition of basic terms

a. **Pronunciation:** Refers to the student's ability to produce understandable statements based on individual sound production, appropriate logical connection of words, and the use of stress and intonation to convey intended meaning. (Thornbury, 2006).

b. **Comprehension: A** component of oral expression that assesses the ability to integrate the explicit implications and meanings of words and sentences in spoken language. This skill includes auditory attention, memory and perception, as well as actual comprehension. (Thornbury, 2006).

c. **Fluency:** Refers to the ability to speak with ease and spontaneity. The student speaks coherently using appropriate sentence length speed. (Thornbury, 2006).

d. **Speech Mastery:** Component of oral expression that evaluates the ability to express ideas and opinions in a coherent and logical discourse using accurate and complex structures according to different statements or situations. (Thornbury, 2006).

e. **Speech.** He must have his own particular technique, showing above all serenity, that he is master of himself. He must speak without haste, giving each word and each sentence its proper intonation. When you reach the climax of your speech, do it with a vibrant voice and with appropriate movements of the whole body. (Porro, 1984)

f. **The conversation**. It consists of one person talking to another, several people talking to each other. In order to be a good conversationalist, one must know how to listen with interest, allowing our interlocutor to finish expressing himself. Hearing is not the same as listening, for while listening is a passive and automatic act, listening requires action and brings into play the whole circuit of thought. Conversation is also called dialogue when several people alternate in the use of the word. Dialogue, prepared according to its form and intention, receives different names. (Porro, 1984)

g. **The interview.** Which usually takes place in front of certain people in the world: politicians, artists, scientists. The interview may be conducted by one or more interviewers, usually journalists or representatives of institutions who, either orally or by reading, ask questions about activities, plans and opinions. It is a dialogue between two people, prepared in advance by one of them (interviewer), in the form of questions addressed to another (interviewee). Its intention is to make known the opinions or personality of the interviewee or through answers. Any subject can be covered and the topics are often varied. (Porro, 1984)

h. **Oral comprehension**. It is a process of receiving what the sender actually expresses (the receptive orientation); constructing and representing meaning (the constructive orientation); negotiating meaning with the sender and responding (the collaborative orientation); and creating meaning through participation, imagination, and empathy (the transformative orientation). (Porro, 1984).

i. **Pronunciation.** Pronunciation means giving the right phonetic value to each word, phrase or sentence, which conditions the quality of communication. (Mamani, 2016).

j. **Oral communication**. O'Maley and Valdez (1996, p. 49) consider that "oral communication refers to the ability to exchange meanings between two or more individuals that are related to the context where the conversation occurs". Therefore, it involves two or more people in an act of conversational exchange.

CHAPTER II

MATERIAL AND METHODS

2.1. Systems of variables

2.1.1. Variable 01: Speaking level

Conceptual definition : Díaz y Ruiz (2008) proposes oral expression as a communicative skill that is executed during the process of social interaction, through the oral emission of a message, with the purpose of exteriorizing and transmitting meanings, which acquires its own and different characteristics in each person, according to their knowledge and needs.

Operational definition

It is the manifestation through pronunciation, fluency, understanding and mastery of speech.

Operational

Variable 01	Dimensions	Indicators	Rating Scale
Speaking English	Pronunciation	➢ Use pronunciation rules ➢ Word Articulation ➢ Sound Intonation	
	Fluidity	➢ Speaks with appropriate fluency ➢ Rarely presents repetition ➢ Uses lexicon	Very good (17-20) Well (13-16) Regular (11-12) Deficient (0-10)
	Understanding	➢ Understands everything perfectly ➢ Question Formulation ➢ Formulation of answers	
	Mastery of Speech	➢ Remarkable use of vocabulary ➢ Use of complex structures ➢ Use of grammatical resources.	

2.2. Research Hypothesis (H1)

2.2.1. General hypothesis

There are differences in the level of oral expression of the English language between students in a public educational institution and a private institution, 2019.

2.2.2. Specific assumptions

The level of oral expression of the English language in students of a public educational institution, 2019 is regular

The level of oral expression of the English language in students of a private educational institution, 2019 is good

2.3. Type of research method

2.3.1 Type of research

According to its purpose

It is applied, given that they are aimed at knowing the level of expression of the English language or aspect of reality belonging to the domain of study of a specific scientific discipline (Channels F and others, 1989)

According to its prolongation in time:

Transversal, because the study corresponds to the recording and comparison of data observed and analyzed at the same time.

According to the emphasis on the nature of the data:

Quantitative: The product that the study data is based on the quantification and calculation of the same (Rodríguez J.P. and others, 2008).

2.3.2   Level of investigation:

Descriptive: It aims to answer the characteristics and conditions in which a phenomenon occurs, or why two or more variables are related (Sánchez Carlessi H. and Reyes Meza C; 2006).

2.4   Research design

The research design can be defined as a schematic structure or organization adopted by the researcher to relate and control the study variables.

The descriptive comparative design allows for the identification of differences or similarities in the distribution of a variable in two or more samples (Hernández, Fernández and Baptista, 1991, p. 158)

The research design is NOT experimental of a comparative descriptive type

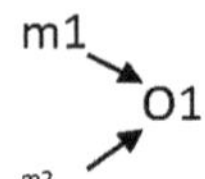

Where:

O1: Correlation Coefficient

m1: 3rd grade students from public high school

m2: 3rd grade students of private educational institution

2.5.   Population and sample

2.5.1.   Population

According to Carrasco (2009), he defines population as: "the set of all the elements (units of analysis) that belong to the spatial scope where the research work is carried out" (p. 237).

The population and sample will be made up of the total number of students at the secondary level, which totals 86, divided as follows.

Educational Institution	Population
0620 - Application (3rd secondary)	64
Values and Science (3rd grade)	28
Total	92

2.5.2. Sample

The sample will be made up of the total number of third grade students at the secondary level in both institutions.

Educational Institution	Population
0620 - Application	29
Values and Science	28
Total	86

CHAPTER III

RESEARCH FINDINGS

Instruments

Questionnaire to measure the level of oral expression of the English language.

Instrument data sheet

Name: Test of oral expression of the English language.

Author: Own elaboration.

Origin: Tarapoto, Peru, 2019.

Objective: To measure the oral expression of the English language.

Administration: Individual.

Duration: Approximately one teaching hour.

Application: 56 third grade high school students

Structure: The instrument consists of 06 questions. It has been considered for the measurement scale, in a dichotomous way as correct (1) and incorrect (0). The final evaluation will be given according to the score obtained in each skill.

The reliability of the instrument will be established through Cronbach's alphas for the entire scale. In the case of validation, this will be done through expert judgement

Data processing and analysis techniques

Authorization will be requested from the director of the educational institution, as well as from the classroom tutors, in order to provide adequate information on the study. Then, with the authorization of the directors of the educational institution, the students will be visited in the respective classrooms where they will be given instructions on the informed procedure and the filling out of the scale.

Descriptive statistics will be used for the adequate data analysis, with which graphic results and the respective tables will be obtained. Finally, the report of the results obtained will be made.

3.1   Contrasting hypotheses.

3.1.1. General hypothesis

For the comparative analysis, we take into account the general objective To determine the differences in the level of oral expression of the English language between students of a public educational institution and a private institution, 2019.

We make use of descriptive statistics

Table No. 01.
Differences in the level of oral expression of the English language between students in a public educational institution and a private institution, 2019

Speaking level	Public	Private
Very good	10.00%	32.14%
Well	20.00%	39.29%
Regular	36.67%	17.86%
Deficient	33.33%	10.71%
TOTAL	100.00%	100.00%

Source. Own preparation based on results

We can identify that students from private institutions have a higher level of oral expression of the English language, in the very good level it is presented with 32.14%, unlike students from public EI where the level of very good oral expression is only 10.00%. In the good level, the comparison shown in Table 01 and Graph 01 is 39.29% for the private institution and 20.00% for the public institution.

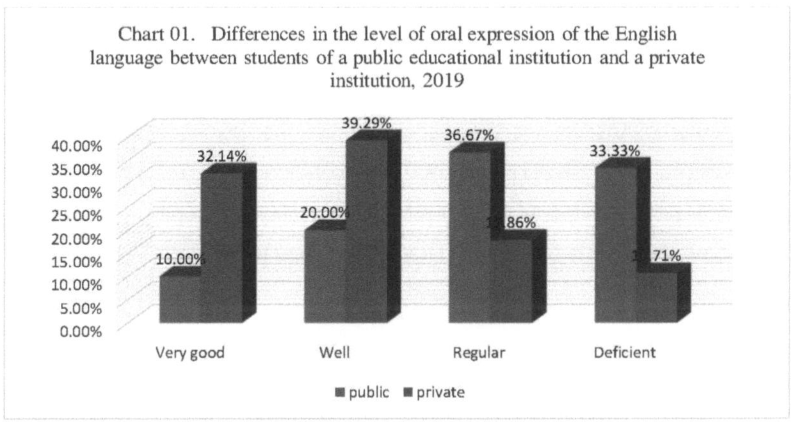

Chart 01. Differences in the level of oral expression of the English language between students of a public educational institution and a private institution, 2019

Source. Own preparation based on results

3.1.2. Specific hypotheses

First hypothesis specifies

For the descriptive analysis, we considered the specific objective 01 To identify the level of oral expression of the English language in students of a public educational institution, 2019.

Then we consider the descriptive reference table.

Table No. 02.
Level of spoken English among students in a public educational institution, 2019.

Speaking level	Frequency	Percentage
Very good	3	10.00%
Well	6	20.00%
Regular	11	36.67%
Deficient	10	33.33%
TOTAL	30	100.00%

Source. Own preparation based on results

Table No. 02 and graph 02 show the level of oral expression of the English language in students of a public educational institution, 2019; the most predominant is the regular level with 36.67%, which indicates that students lead do not understand everything perfectly, difficulties in formulating questions, little use of vocabulary, little use of complex structures and grammatical resources.

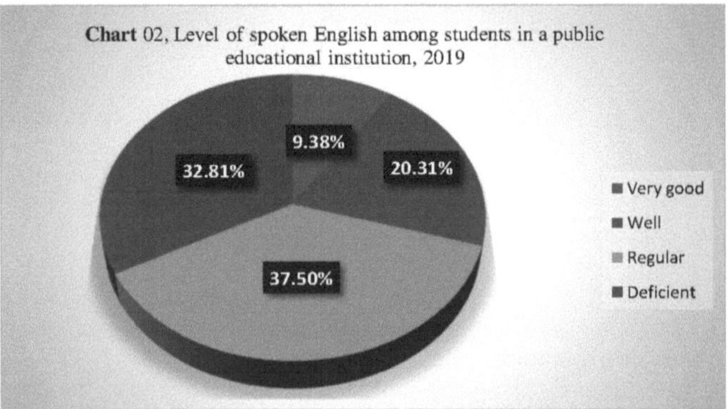

Source. Own preparation based on results

Second specific scenario

For the descriptive analysis, we considered the specific objective 02 To identify the level of oral expression of the English language in students of a private educational institution, 2019.

Then we considered the reference table.

Table No. 03.
Level of spoken English among students in a private educational institution, 2019.

Speaking level	Frequency	Percentage
Very good	9	32.14%
Well	11	39.29%
Regular	5	17.86%
Deficient	3	10.71%
TOTAL	28	100.00%

Source. Own preparation based on results

Table No. 03 and graph No. 03 show that the level of oral expression of the English language in students in a private educational institution, 2019, is at the level of 39.9%, which indicates that students present better conditions in word articulation, intonation of sounds, speaking with appropriate fluency and rarely present repetition. The very good level is at 32.14% and the regular level at 17.86%,

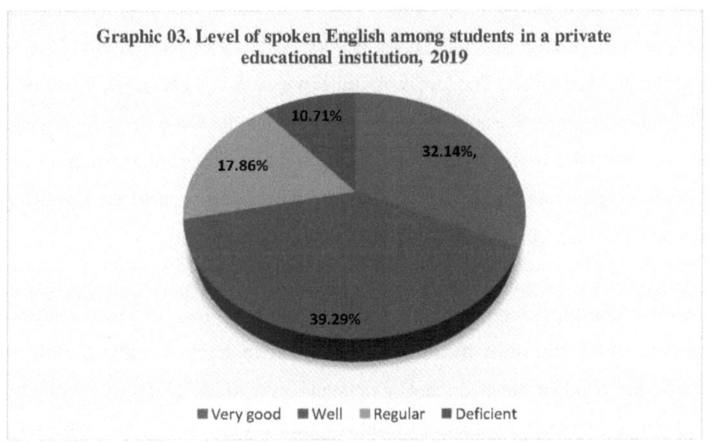

Source. Own preparation based on results

Discussion of results

It was concluded that the private institutions have a higher level of oral expression of the English language, in the very good level it is presented with 32.14%, unlike the students of the public EI where the level of very good oral expression is only 9.38%. In the good level, the comparison shown in Table 01 and Graph 01 is 39.29% for the private institution and 20.31% for the public institution. In view of this, León (2014) mentioned that the pronunciation, fluency, comprehension and mastery of speech, of the experimental group, were located at the highest levels and showed significant differences (p < 0.05) with respect to those of the control, according to the post-test.

The global average of oral expression in the experimental group, according to the post-test was 16.86 and in the pre-test 11.00. Palomino, Polo and Sedano (2015) found a significant relationship between the study variables. In this sense, teachers should be trained to use educational media to improve oral expression and comprehension. Likewise, Álvarez and Panta (2017) concluded that in pronunciation, fluency, comprehension and command of the oral expression of the English language in the control group, according to the post-test, indicate that there was some improvement in oral expression, placing the students in the low levels of evaluation, that is to say, in the regular and bad levels. The levels of oral expression in each one of its dimensions: pronunciation, comprehension, fluency and command of the speech, revealed an important difference between the control group and the experimental group, so we have that in the experimental group the results in pronunciation reached the highest levels: excellent, (35.71%); very good, (35.71%) and good (28.57%).

The level of oral expression of the English language in students of a public educational institution, 2019; the most predominant is the regular level with 37.50%, which indicates that students lead do not understand everything perfectly, difficulties in formulating questions. The deficient level is found with 32.81%.   In contrast, Quispe (2017) found that students in the third grade of secondary school at the El Mártir José Olaya de Ventanilla educational institution develop oral English language proficiency in a sub-optimal manner; what they do best is in oral comprehension, but they have greater difficulty in oral expression.   In turn, Aspajo (2014), found that they are between the levels of deficient and poor, without finding participants in the levels of regular, good and very good. In that sense, Ramírez (2017) found that students express themselves orally, allowing the teacher to have a broader conceptual and cognitive vision when applying techniques that allow the development of oral expression of English.

The level of oral expression of the English language in students from a private educational institution, 2019, is at 39.9%, which indicates that students have better conditions in the articulation of words. The very good level is at 32.14% and the regular level at 17.86%. On the other hand, Palma and Zapata (2017) concluded that 87% of students in the third grade of secondary school show a low level of oral expression, as evidenced by the results. The learning sessions were designed taking into account the different methodological strategies, which led us to improve oral expression.   In turn, Mamani (2016) indicates that students managed to reach high levels (good and very good) in the development of their oral expression skills, as a result of the application of cooperative learning, this in the experimental group, while in the control group, students remain at the levels of regular and good. In addition, Navarro and Zarate (2016) found that Students have limitations in solving real life communicative tasks, according to their educational level; and the different educational activities, whose purpose is the progress and mastery in the area of English, show a serious interruption and an intermittent flow that makes it impossible to apprehend knowledge.

CONCLUSIONS

It was concluded that the private institutions have a higher level of oral expression of the English language, in the very good level it is presented with 32.14%, unlike the students of the public EI where the level of very good oral expression is only 9.38%. In the good level, the comparison shown in Table 01 and Graph 01 is 39.29% for the private institution and 20.31% for the public institution.

The level of oral expression of the English language in students of a public educational institution, 2019; the most predominant is the regular level with 37.50%, which indicates that students lead do not understand everything perfectly, difficulties in formulating questions. The deficient level is found with 32.81%.

The level of oral expression of the English language in students from a private educational institution, 2019, is at 39.9%, which indicates that students have better conditions in the articulation of words. The very good level is at 32.14% and the regular level at 17.86%,

RECOMMENDATIONS

- To the directors of public educational institutions, encourage their teachers to develop programs to improve the level of oral expression, considering the experiences and lessons learned from private education.

- To teachers of the English language, to guide their students and parents in the different techniques and strategies that allow them to achieve greater expression ora in order to facilitate the process of learning the English language of the students.

- Classroom teachers employ English language teaching techniques and strategies that motivate students to learn the foreign language and thus improve the level of oral expression of the English language.

BIBLIOGRAPHIC REFERENCES

Álvarez, L. and Panta, S. (2017). The application of the role-play technique to improve the oral expression of the English language in students in the fifth year of secondary school at the Manuel Muñoz Najar educational institution, Arequipa - 2016. Degree thesis. Universidad Nacional de San Agustín de Arequipa - Faculty of Educational Sciences

I suck. (2014). Techniques to develop the capacity of oral expression and comprehension in the learning of the English language. Iquitos: National University of the Peruvian Amazon.

Bakken, A. S., & Lund, R. E. (2018). Why should learners of English read? Norwegian English teachers' notions of EFL reading. Teaching and Teacher Education, 70, 78–87. https://doi.org/10.1016/j.tate.2017.11.002.

Bañuelos, C. (2014). A study on the oral production of the English language. Faculty of Languages UABC Tijuana Mexico. Undergraduate thesis.

Brown, G. y Yule, G. (1983). Teaching the spoken language. New York: Cambridge University Press.

Bygates, M. (1991), Speaking. United Kingdom: Oxford University Press.

Byrne, D. (1989). Teaching Oral English. England: Longman Group UK limited.

Council of Europe. (2001). the Common European Framework of Reference for Languages: Learning, Teaching, Assessment. Council of Europe, 1–273. https://doi.org/10.1017/S0267190514000221UNESCO, 2016).

Diaz, Garcia. & Ruiz. (2008). Alternative curriculum to encourage the development of oral expression in primary school students. Cuba: University

Fonseca, M. (2005). Oral communication. Fundamentals and strategic practice. Mexico: Pearson. Retrieved from https://espacioculturayarte.files.wordpress.com/2016/05/comunicacion-oral.pdf

Fuertes, N; Escudero, I; Armijos, J and Loaiza, E. (2018). Synergy of active methods in oral expression, grammar and vocabulary in students of English as a foreign language. Espacios Magazine. Vol. 39 (N° 35) Year 2018. P. 31.

Guamán, V. (2014). Verbal games and their impact on oral expression. UTA. 123 p. Ambato, Ecuador.

Harmer, J. (2000). The practice of English Language Teaching. Harlow: Longman.

Leon. G. (2014). Participatory techniques to improve the oral expression of the English language. Case: mechatronics students from SENATI, de la Esperanza-Trujillo. Academic cycle 2013-II. Private University Antenor Orrego Postgraduate School Postgraduate section of technical education.

Littlewood, W. (1994).Communicative Language Teaching. Recuperado de https://books.google.es/books?id=LRataYhTQ3gC&hl=es&source=gbs_book_other_ versions.

Mamani, E.(2016). The cooperative learning as a strategy in the development of the oral expression in English in the students of the Tourism School of UNA Puno 2016. National University of the Altiplano Faculty of Educational Sciences. Second specialization program

Medina A. (2012). Language Didactics: How to teach English and Spanish with a competence approach? Cuba: Author's edition

Ministry of National Education. (2012). Foreign language English. Curricular basis. Colombia: Espantapájaros Taller (Scarecrow Workshop).

MINEDU (2017). Ministry of Education of Peru. Retrieved October 29, 2017, from Programa curricular- Educación Secundaria: http://www.minedu.gob.pe/curriculo/pdf/programacurricular- educacion- secundaria.pdf

Navarro. H: and Zarate, W. (2016). Difficulties presented by students in the oral production of English in the fifth grade of Max Planck High School. Diploma thesis. Universidad de la Salle faculty of educational sciences degree in Spanish, English and French. Colombia.

O'malley, M. y Pierce, L. (1996): Authentic assessment for English language learners: practical approaches for teachers. Nueva York: Addison Wesley.

O'Maley y Valdez. (1996). The practice of comunicacion teaching elt 124. Oxford: Pergamen Oxford.

Palma, E. and Zapata, C. (2017). Methodological strategies to improve oral expression in the area of English, of 3rd grade students of the I.E.E. "Juan Manuel Iturregui" - Province of Lambayeque. Degree thesis. Faculty of historical social sciences and education program of academic complementation. National University "Pedro Ruiz Gallo"

Palomino, K; Polo, R .and Sedano, J. (2015). Educational media and the oral expression and comprehension of English in third grade students of the experimental application school of the National University of Education Enrique Guzmán y Valle, Chosica, 2015. Diploma thesis. Enrique Guzmán y Valle National University of Education.

Pomposo, L. (2016). The evaluation of oral competence in second languages. The case of English in the professional world. English Department. Faculty of Education, Camilo José Cela University, Madrid. Didactics. Language and Literature. 2016, vol. 28, 243-262   ISSN: 1130-0531.   http://dx.doi.org/10.5209/DIDA.54091.

Porro, M. (1984). Spontaneous forms of oral expression in Spanish language practice (p.25). Havana: People and education.

Quispe, W. (2017). Oral English language proficiency in third grade students at El Mártir José Olaya de Ventanilla educational institution, 2016. Diploma thesis. Cesar Vallejo University. Faculty of education and languages

Richards, J. C., & Reppen, R. (2014). Towards a pedagogy of grammar instruction. RELC Journal, 45(1), 5–25. https://doi.org/10.1177/0033688214522622.

Richards, J. y Rodger, T. (2001). Approaches and Methods in Language Teachin. Second edition Cambridge: Cambridge University Press

Ramírez, B. (2017). The linguistic games for the development of the oral expression of the English language in the students of the secondary section of the New Vision School in the period 2015 - 2016. Degree thesis.

Thornbury, S. (2006). How to teach Speaking. Recuperado de https://es.scribd.com/doc/275587410/Thornbury-How-to-Teach-Speaking-pdf

Ur, P. (1996). A course in language teaching. Practice and theory. Cambridge: Cambridge University Press.

Vygotsky, S. (1987). History of the development of higher psychic functions and communication. Retrieved from http://www.ibe.unesco.org/sites/default/files/vygotskys.PDF..

Attachments:

The following is the order of the annexes:

Annex 1: Data collection instruments.

Annex 2: Consistency matrix

Annex 1

Data collection instrument

English Speaking Questionnaire

Name:.. Section:.......................

Dear student:

The purpose of this questionnaire is to find out how you are developing your English language learning process. Please read each item carefully and answer as honestly and objectively as possible. The statements have several possibilities of answer and you must choose and mark with a cross (x) the frequency with which you carry out the following actions. N°

ORAL EXPRESSION

1. I clearly express my personal data, activities I like and hobbies using the English language.

2. I participate in dialogues about greetings, presentations and professions during the English class.

3. I exchange ideas, opinions and information with my colleagues or the teacher in the English language.

4. I answer information questions clearly.

5. I ask my classmates questions in English about pictures, drawings, observed photographs and they understand me.

6. When I speak in English, my classmates easily understand what I'm saying

TITLE	PROBLEM	OBJECTIVES	HYPOTHESIS	VARIABLE	DIMENSIONS	INDICATORS	RATING SCALE	METHODOLOGY
"English Language Speaking Level in Students at a Public and Private Educational Institution, 2019"	What differences do we find between the level of oral expression of the English language in students of a public and private educational institution, 2019? **Specific questions** -What is the level of oral expression of the English language in students of a public educational institution, 2019? -What is the level of oral expression of the English language in students of a private educational institution, 2019?	**Overall objective** To determine the differences in the level of oral expression of the English language between students in a public educational institution and a private institution, 2019. **Specific Objectives** Identify the level of English language expression in students at a public educational institution, 2019 Identify the level of oral expression of the English language in students of a private educational institution, 2019	**Research Hypothesis** **General hypothesis** There are differences in the level of oral expression of the English language between students in a public educational institution and a private institution, 2019. **Specific hypotheses** The level of oral expression of the English language in students of a public educational institution, 2019 is regular The level of oral expression of the English language in students of a private educational institution, 2019 is good	Oral expression	Pronunciation Fluidity Understanding Mastery of Speech	➤ Use pronunciation rules ➤ Word Articulation ➤ Sound Intonation ➤ Speaks with appropriate fluency ➤ Rarely presents repetition ➤ Uses lexicon ➤ Understands everything perfectly ➤ Question Formulation ➤ Formulation of answers ➤ Remarkable use of vocabulary ➤ Use of complex structures ➤ Use of grammar resources	Very good (17-20) Well (13-16) Regular (11-12) Deficient (0-10)	**Type of Research** Applicable because it is based on a theoretical context to know, describe, relate or explain a reality, according to Mejía, Elías. **Research Level** According to Danhke's classification, quoted by Hernández, Fernández and Baptista (2003), the research belongs to the descriptive level, because it tries to describe the conditions in which a variable is presented. **Research Design.** This type of research is of the Descriptive - comparative type, whose scheme is as follows: m1 ↘ O1 m2 ↗ Where: O1: Correlation Coefficient m1: students of a public educational institution m2: students from a private educational institution

Buy your books fast and straightforward online - at one of world's fastest growing online book stores! Environmentally sound due to Print-on-Demand technologies.

Buy your books online at
www.morebooks.shop

Kaufen Sie Ihre Bücher schnell und unkompliziert online – auf einer der am schnellsten wachsenden Buchhandelsplattformen weltweit! Dank Print-On-Demand umwelt- und ressourcenschonend produzi ert.

Bücher schneller online kaufen
www.morebooks.shop

KS OmniScriptum Publishing
Brivibas gatve 197
LV-1039 Riga, Latvia
Telefax: +371 686 204 55

info@omniscriptum.com
www.omniscriptum.com

Printed by Books on Demand GmbH, Norderstedt / Germany